Be the TOP TIPS

cing

Rebecca Rissman

Raintree

www.raintreepublishers.co.uk
Visit our website to find out
more information about
Raintree books.

To order:
☎ Phone 0845 6044371
📄 Fax +44 (0) 1865 312263
💻 Email myorders@raintreepublishers.co.uk

Customers from outside the UK please telephone +44 1865 312262

Raintree is an imprint of Capstone Global Library
Limited, a company incorporated in England and
Wales having its registered office at 7 Pilgrim Street,
London, EC4V 6LB – Registered company number:
6695582

Text © Capstone Global Library Limited 2013
First published in hardback in 2013
First published in paperback in 2014
The moral rights of the proprietor have been
asserted.

Edited by Rebecca Rissman, Dan Nunn, and
 Adrian Vigliano
Designed by Joanna Hinton-Malivoire
Original illustrations © Capstone Global Library Ltd
Picture research by Ruth Blair
Originated by Capstone Global Library
Printed in China by CTPS

ISBN 978 1 406 24108 2 (hardback)
16 15 14 13 12
10 9 8 7 6 5 4 3 2 1

ISBN 978 1 406 24113 6 (paperback)
17 16 15 14 13
10 9 8 7 6 5 4 3 2 1

British Library Cataloguing in Publication Data
A full catalogue record for this book is available
from the British Library.

Acknowledgements
The author and publishers are grateful to the
following for permission to reproduce copyright
material: Shutterstock pp. 5 (© Yuri Arcurs), 6 (©
Catalin Petolea), 9 (© bogdanhoda), 10 (© Tusia),
12 (© Quang Ho), 14 (© Karel Gallas), 16 (© Alta
Oosthuizen), 21 (© Tan, Kim Pin), 25 (© Volodymyr
Goinyk), 27 (© AVAVA), 29 (© Vladimir Gerasimov),
29 (© photolinc), 30 (© Robert Anthony), 18 (©
Picsfive), 19 (© Kamira). Background and design
features reproduced with the permission of
Shutterstock.

Cover photograph reproduced with the permission
of Shutterstock and Shutterstock/© notkoo.

We would like to thank Nancy Harris for her
invaluable help in the preparation of this book.

Every effort has been made to contact copyright
holders of any material reproduced in this book.
Any omissions will be rectified in subsequent
printings if notice is given to the publisher.

Some words are shown in bold, **like this**. You can find
out what they mean by looking in the glossary.

Contents

Get going!

People write every day. **Emails**, or computer messages, notes, and letters are all things we write. But sometimes writing can seem tricky. Don't worry, this book is full of tips to make writing easy and fun!

Help!

Today I...

Top Tip

Get going! The more you write, the easier it will become. Try writing 15 minutes every day. You could write in a journal about what you did during the day.

5

Imagine your reader

Before you write anything, stop and ask yourself: "Who am I writing for?" You might write a letter to your teacher in one way, or **style**. You might write to your best friend in a different style.

Top Tip

Think about who you are writing for before you start to write!

Test that tip!

How would you begin an **email**, or computer message, to your head teacher?

- Hey dude,
- What's up?
- Dear Mrs Miller,

Think it through

What do you want to write about? Writing about something you are interested in will make it more fun and exciting. Deciding on your **topic**, or subject, before you get started will also help you prepare to write.

Top Tip

Decide what you want to write about before you get started!

Test that tip!

Which of these topics is most exciting to you?

- Monster trucks
- Bicycle races

Choose one and write a story!

But why?

The reason you are writing might determine the way you write. Ask yourself: "Why am I writing this?"

Top Tip
Think about the **purpose**, or reason, for your writing.

Test that tip!

Here are some reasons you might be writing:

- to explain something
- to tell how to make something
- to describe something
- to tell a story
- to tell someone your thoughts or opinion about something.

Many options

You've decided *what* you want to write about and *why* you are writing. It is now time to think about *how* you want to write! There are many different **genres**, or types, of writing.

Ooops!

Top Tip

Think about your reader and your **topic**, or subject, when you decide on a genre.

Test that tip!

Here is a list of genres:

?

Explanation text	information or facts about real things
Narrative text	a make-believe or **fiction** story
Discussion text	your opinion or thoughts about something
Instruction text	how to do or make something

The write stuff!

Before you start writing, you need to get your thoughts and questions **organized**, or in order. This is a good time to let your thoughts go wild! This is called **brainstorming**.

?

Top Tip

When brainstorming, make a list of all the words, questions, and ideas you have about your topic. Then, go through your list and narrow it down to the best ideas.

Test that tip!

Giraffes

Mammal

Long neck

Grasslands

How tall are giraffes?

How do they sleep?

What do they eat?

Outline it!

Outlines are useful tools to use when writing. You can use them like a map to practise laying out what you'll write.

Top Tip

Use outlines to lay out what you want to write.

Test that tip!

Giraffes book report outline:

What are giraffes?
   Mammals

What do giraffes look like?
   Tall
   Long necks
   Spotted

Where do giraffes live?
   Grasslands

How do giraffes behave?

Draft time

When you're ready to start writing, first write a **draft**, or rough version. Just write down what you want to write about. Don't worry about how your writing looks. Drafts can be messy!

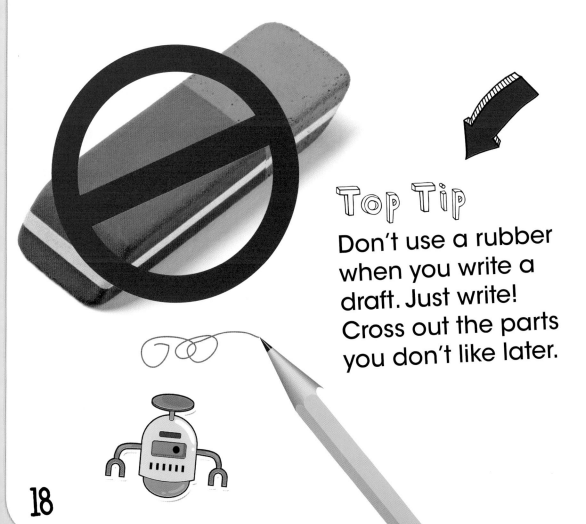

Top Tip

Don't use a rubber when you write a draft. Just write! Cross out the parts you don't like later.

18

Revise it!

After you have written your **draft**, or rough version, read through it and look for things you like. Then try to rewrite, or **revise**, the parts you didn't like.

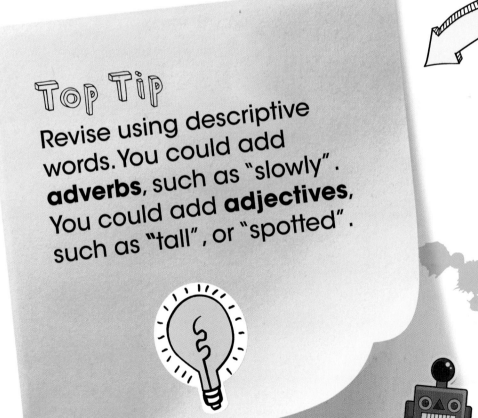

Top Tip

Revise using descriptive words. You could add **adverbs**, such as "slowly". You could add **adjectives**, such as "tall", or "spotted".

Test that tip!

First draft

~~The giraffe ate its food.~~

~~There was a giraffe standing by the tree.~~

Revised draft

The giraffe moved slowly as it ate its food.

There was a tall, spotted giraffe standing by the tree.

Punctuate it!

As you **edit**, or correct, your writing, make sure to **punctuate** your writing. Punctuation marks, such as full stops and question marks, tell people how to read what you have written.

Top Tip

! Use a ! to show that something is exciting.

? Use a ? to show that a question is being asked.

. Use a . to finish a sentence.

" " Use "" to show that someone is talking.

, Use a , to tell your reader to pause, or when you are listing items.

Test that tip!

How would you punctuate this sentence?

My birds are chirping

Spell it out!

Another **editing** tip is to correct your spelling. Words that are misspelled can confuse your reader.

Top Tip

Always have a dictionary and **thesaurus** nearby. Dictionaries will help you to spell correctly. Thesauruses will help you find the best words to use.

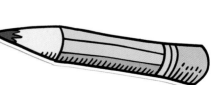

Test that tip!

Use a dictionary to find which of these words is misspelled:

- iceberg
- teenager
- spoted

Finishing touches

When you're ready, it's time to finish what you've written. You'll want to make sure it's ready for other people to read. Read through your writing again. If you need to, copy or type it out to make it easy to read.

Top Tip

Before you hand in a school writing assignment, don't forget to include:

- Your name
- A title
- The date

Study like a pro!

Set yourself up to succeed by practising these tips when you study or do your homework.

Top Tip

Before you start work, always:

- ⇒ Eat a healthy snack
- ⇒ Turn off the television
- ⇒ Make sure you have all the supplies you need:
  - books
  - dictionary
  - **thesaurus**, or resource for finding more words to use
  - highlighter
  - pencil and rubber

Dream big!

Remember, writing can be useful in many ways as you grow up! You can use it in your job as a journalist, musician, chef, or lawyer. You might even write a best-selling book that people around the world can enjoy!

What can you do to become a better writer today?

Glossary

adjective describing word. Adjectives describe nouns.

adverb describing word. Adverbs describe verbs.

brainstorming way to quickly come up with new ideas. Brainstorming can be very messy and fun.

discussion genre that communicates the writer's opinion or thoughts about something. For example, whether something is good or bad, funny or sad, and so on.

draft non-final version of something. Many writers like to write a rough draft, first draft, and final draft of a paper.

edit to correct or improve upon something

email electronic message sent or received online

explanation genre that teaches you about a topic

fiction about imaginary events or people

genre category of writing, such as narrative, discussion, or instruction

instruction genre that shows you how to do something

narrative genre that tells a story

organized kept in a neat order

outline rough framework for a piece of writing

punctuation symbols that help the reader understand the text

purpose reason for doing something

revise edit to make something more clear or neat

style way of writing something. Some styles are funny, scary, or bossy.

thesaurus tool that shows you what words mean the same or similar things. You can use a thesaurus to find interesting new words to use in your writing.

topic subject

Find out more

Books

I Can Write (series), Anita Ganeri (Raintree, 2012)

Oxford Primary Dictionary, Oxford Dictionaries (Oxford University Press, 2011)

Oxford Junior Thesaurus, Oxford Dictionaries (Oxford University Press, 2012)

Websites

www.bbc.co.uk/schools/ks2bitesize/english
Visit the BBC Bitesize English website for help and advice with reading, writing, spelling and grammar, plus interactive games, quizzes, and lots of other activities.

www.scholastic.com/dogslife/createtale.htm
Set the scene and create a story about a dog at this site!

Index